CLASSIC AIRCRAFT MOODS

AIRS & GRACES

MARTIN W. BOWMAN

HALSGROVE

First published in Great Britain in 2005

Title page: *Tora! Tora! Tora!*

British Library Cataloguing-in-Publication Data
A CIP record for this title is available from the British Library

ISBN 1 84114 352 9

HALSGROVE
Halsgrove House
Lower Moor Way
Tiverton, Devon EX16 6SS
T: 01884 243242
F: 01884 243325
email: sales@halsgrove.com
website: www.halsgrove.com

Printed and bound by D'Auria Industrie Grafiche Spa, Italy

CONTENTS

Ferocious Frankie

THE TRAILER
INTRODUCTION BY MARTIN W. BOWMAN

'Taking air-to-airs is easy!' After all digi cameras and auto-focus, auto-wind and auto everything are almost idiot proof, so surely all you have to do, once you've settled in behind your pilot, is point and shoot? Why, anyone could do it, even my grandmother with a Kodak Brownie I hear you say!

But could they? First you have to get up there.

Of one thing we are all agreed. It is said that a picture tells a thousand words. It takes thousands of words and hundreds of volumes to describe the world of military, sport and commercial aviation history and the achievements of the many. In this pictorial indulgence, which was shot in over twenty countries from Australia to Africa, Greenland to Great Britain and the USA to the USSR I have attempted to conjure up some delicacies from the feast available to anyone with a camera and an interest in using it.

The majority of images were rehearsed and choreographed before take off with face-to-face briefings where the photographer asks what he would ideally like to do and the pilot(s) say whether it is practical and safe to do it. (I was once labelled very lucky to see a Spitfire off my wing to photograph – he honestly thought we had a chance rendezvous in the sky and that it was not pre-planned!). Normally a pilot asks, 'where do you want me/us?' If there are two or more aircraft involved it is often expedient to ask one of the pilots to fly nearest the camera and then have him change position. While they are carrying out this rehearsed manoeuvre you have time to readjust, change film/cameras or whatever. I always ask that they 'fly on the sunny side of the street'. Above all they must be in close, very close. As American war photographer Robert Capa of *Life* magazine said, 'If your photos are not good enough you are not close enough.' He ought to know. Capa went in with the initial assault on *Omaha* Beach on D-Day.

If you have to resort to a lens longer than 35mm then forget it. Go and do something easy like joining the commandos.

Luck sometimes plays a part in the proceedings but you also have to be alert to opportunities. Some of the images herein have been shot purely by chance when an opportunity presented itself. At Lakeland, Florida prior to take off the pilot of P-51D Mustang *Petie 2nd* was running through his cockpit check positioned beside a large puddle for the perfect reflection shot. Luckily he was positioned down-sun but he was oblivious to the fabulous photo-opportunity it presented. Running like crazy across the airfield I just managed to record the shot for posterity before the pilot released the brakes and taxied out!

It's a special feeling being a fly-on-the-wall cameraman occupying the jump seat of a B-52 and in C-130 heading for Mogadishu and aboard a Herc skirting the Alps en route to Sarajevo during the war in Bosnia. But you are not a fly on the wall at all. You are in harm's way and if your luck is out you're one of the flies that gets squashed.

Then there is always the unexpected.

What began as a routine air-to-air session with a Ryan PT-22 one Remembrance Sunday ended in disaster. The photo of the Ryan, taken from a de Havilland Chipmunk, is the last one ever of this aircraft. The plan was for the Ryan to join in formation with a Stearman but a few minutes after this photograph was taken the Ryan developed engine trouble and crashed in a recently-harvested sugar beet field at Pudding Norton near Fakenham, Norfolk. The pilot in the rear cockpit skillfully dug the left wing into the ground to soften the crash landing and he and his passenger were able to scramble out and walk away with nothing worse than cuts and bruises.

Although it is historically accurate and photogenic for pilots of Warbirds to be pictured wearing WW2-style flying helmets, bone-domes lessen the chance of serious head injuries. A bone dome is not a legal requirement unless you are flying in jet aircraft but it will probably save your life if the engine fails and you have to crash land. (In crashes pilots have been killed hitting the instrument panel in WW2 leather helmets).

If you are not a pilot by profession then flight suits can look flash and many egotists like wearing them festooned with badges! However, flight suits are a must for an air-to-air

photo-shoot. You can never have enough pockets for cameras, camera lens and spare batteries and films (and sick bags?). Once you are in the air that's it, you can't go back for more of the same. Flight suit pockets are mainly zippered too, so these are a must for putting all loose items in (after strapping in you normally find that only the legging pockets are unobstructed by the straps). If you are going fly with the canopy shut then rip those flashy patches off your flight suit if you don't want to have them reflected in the shot. Similarly, don't wear a white T-shirt either.

Always carry at least two cameras – just in case – but watch the dangling second one; it can easily wedge itself between your lap and the joystick and jam the flight controls. One answer is shortening the length of the camera straps so the camera does not dangle lower than your chest. Move an inch to the left or right in a Yak 52 for instance and one touches the side control sticks. Lean forward an inch to get that shot over the side and you touch the joy stick, which is like a large broom handle sticking into your stomach. Move your feet an inch and you will snag the rudder wires which run parallel along the floor like little trip wires for the unwary. All this is tricky when you are trussed up like a turkey, have two cameras around your neck, and you're hot and the adrenaline is flowing like a torrent as you twist and turn to get that much sought-after shot whilst trying to avoid the glare of the sun and the reflection on your canopy. Then there's that obtrusive wing which stretches out from the fuselage root like Southend Pier. Jam the controls and you'll have to suffer in silence because you can't reach the microphone switch to tell your pilot what a sad so-and-so you are and he is saying, 'Can I have my stick back'?!

Communication with your pilot is a must. A headset microphone is useless, as aerial photographers have to take one hand off the camera to press the 'tit' if they want to speak. (I once had to tell my pilot that I was still there. I had been silent for so long he must have thought I had bailed out!). The arm gets in the way, as does the 'Battle of Britain' type mask with built-in mike, which makes looking through the viewfinder virtually impossible. A helmet with a throat mike is better.

Good photos can depend on what aircraft are being flown, the weather and whether the photographer is having a good day or an off day, and what calibre the pilots are. Pilots are like drivers. Just because you have a driving licence it does not make you a great driver any more than having a great camera makes you a great photographer.

Military pilots and ex-military pilots are peerless when it comes to briefing and formation flying. Flying in jets wing tip to wing tip into ambrosia creamed rice at 1000ft and emerging in the clear blue at 10 000 ft with the same two-feet separation we had when we entered the clag has to be experienced to be believed. The aim of the flight was to try and get a vertical shot of the wingman's Jet Provost Mk3 while looping the loop. I would only attempt this manoeuvre with two experienced jet pilots. Mine was a retired wing commander who has flown Gnats, Hunters and Harriers et al. in a long and distinguished career. His wingman, a retired squadron leader, has an equally distinguished career behind him with more hours on Jaguars than any other pilot. So up we went to 10 000ft, a little high for the elderly JP Mk3, but because of the cloud base we needed to dive to 8000 ft before pulling up to get the shot in the clear. But when we dived down from 10 000 ft and then at 8000 ft pulled up and started climbing, with our wingman mirroring our manoeuvre, I had extreme difficulty lifting the Canon EOS to my eye. (I forgot to mention that the JP Mk3 is not pressurized). Pulling 5G my arms were like lead and the camera had become as heavy as an anvil. It felt like someone had just placed a bag of cement on my chest. My body was giving a good impression of trying to compress itself in my socks! Grunting and groaning I tried valiantly to snap the wingman but as the shutter clicked he darted briefly behind our right wing tip tank – Missed! No time for a second attempt: I couldn't lift the camera up again and anyway that was the last frame (idiot!). My pilot, fresh as a daisy, said I sounded like an old man grunting and groaning in the loop manoeuvre (unlike a propeller driven aircraft, where the G comes off on the downward part of the loop, it stays 'on' in a jet). I had to see the funny side of it. While I could easily give each of these two sixties' steely-eyed killers 15 years, when it comes to flying jets, they are definitely the fitter!

Another ex RAF pilot who comes to mind is one who for many years was an airline captain of note. I often flew with him in Stearmans. He carried a piece of rope and a mobile phone. I know why he carried the mobile. Handy if we force landed somewhere off the beaten track but the rope? 'Never know when you might need it' he said. One afternoon when heavy rain threatened to flood the large cockpits of the Stearmans at the Harrier station he simply tied a cover over the openings and we had the only dry seat in the house flying back home!

During a shoot some pilots instinctively know where they should or could be. Apart from having more hours on Spitfires than any other living pilot, Squadron Leader Paul Day, who until retirement led the BBMF, must have a sixth sense. When I flew aboard the Lancaster and was photographing him in one of the Spitfire XIXs, he noticed me in the radio room widow because he slotted the Spitfire perfectly between the Lanc's outer wing tip and the No.1 Merlin. I had not asked for this unique shot – he just knew! A few pilots (and the photographer on occasion) miss their cue. Sometimes simply flying on the 'sunny side of the street' is still wrong. It is most irritating that some WW2 artists painted the nose art on the wrong side! Trying to photograph the 'Mickey The Moocher' motif into sun because the painting is on the left-hand side of the Lanc whose crew are flying south not north can be tricky.

What is the best camera ship? They all have drawbacks. The tail turret of the Lancaster makes a great camera platform but try taking downward shots of two Spitfires through the

Me and my shadow

cut away panel in the perspex wearing a flight suit, boots, bone dome and visor. You cannot do it sitting down (too low) or standing up (no headroom). You have to grin and bear it and stand with knees bent and the weight on your thighs. Try this for 30 minutes! (And as for a Piper Cub is not the aircraft to fly in if you have just had a vasectomy).

Seriously, if you are not prepared to get into positions where it hurts, stay on the ground.

Normally one cannot just sit in an aircraft and blaze away (although I have done it once or twice in a comfortable airline-style-seat Malibu, and facing backwards too which made it much easier all round). It's not like pulling up your favourite armchair and turning the TV on. The sky is a three-dimensional world and the aerial photographer is more often in a confined and cramped space with no room to manoeuvre. The six seat- and parachute-harness straps have to be tight but they make movement for that rear three-quarter shot almost impossible unless you loosen the shoulder straps. This still leaves the waist straps and negative-G strap under your crotch to consider and the additional trailing camera straps which after a few frames are shot, left and right, right and left... tend to wrap themselves around your neck.

In jet aircraft strapping in means inserting, twisting, coupling and dovetailing ten straps: two of everything, and a negative G strap, which comes up under your crotch. All are then inserted through each other's loops and into a central junction box.

Generally, in a side-by-side seat camera ship it is not always easy when you have to sit in the right hand seat and the subject matter is on the left of the camera ship. In a tandem seat aircraft like the Yak 52 and Harvard it is best to be able to point and shoot over your left shoulder simply because the camera button is on the right (try looking through a viewfinder with the camera over your right shoulder). If the sun is on the 'wrong' side – tough. Ideally you need to get as high as possible with the clouds, if there are any, obscuring

the ground. It is not always possible to do this for several reasons, so make the best of it. Pick out a feature and incorporate it in your 'six'. Watch out for the sun. Clouds will make it appear and disappear as your speeding camera ship traverses the sky. Sometimes shots in bad weather can make you look like a bad photographer but not all shots need to be in blue skies. The only bad photographers are those who leave their cameras at home.

Most would give their eye-teeth to fly in the Lancaster, a B-52 or the *Snowbirds*, but first you have to be prepared to undergo the pre-flight training and safety briefings. The *Snowbirds'* experience begins with a two-hour briefing. My seven other right-seaters were fairly relaxed about everything at first. The instruction 'all passengers must remove makeup and earrings' (oil-based make-up and 100% oxygen is a fire-hazard), even caused amusement. Then the ejection seat sequence was explained, just in case a catastrophic in-flight emergency or ground fire was to occur during your flight. The words, 'Bail out! Bail out!' echoing around the hushed room (which would be the last ones used by your pilot before you were left talking to yourself) really concentrated minds wonderfully. Working details of the PSP (Personal Survival Pack, a yellow box under your backside, stirred imaginations further. We were reliably told that after ejection we should discard the PSP before landing but if we were heading for a pine forest, then it was best to keep it attached as it was useful for glancing your body off a jack pine! One or two looked ready to use their 'boarding passes' (euphemism for 'sick bags') now.

There are no special qualifications for flying in passenger jets but a unique check in procedure is required before one can fly aboard a mighty B-52H sitting on the fold-down jump seat on the cramped flight deck. A whole day is spent in 'egress training' learning how to operate the pilot and navigator ejection seats (they are different) and other emergency procedures. Also, some prospective jump-seaters can get claustrophobia when they don the lightweight bone dome and oxygen mask so egress training includes an oxygen-breathing test wearing this equipment. If you fail you will not make the flight. One wears the same forty-pound parachute backpack that the pilots and navigators wear. (When wearing a parachute pack the Yak-52 is an uncomfortable and cramped aircraft though there is more legroom in a B-52 than a Yak 52 – just!) If in an in-flight emergency you were told to evacuate the B-52 you would disconnect oxygen and intercom, undo the seat belt and shin down the pole behind to the navigator compartment below and bale out through one of the holes left by the downward firing ejection seats. (If an ejection fails, the occupant can vacate the seat – with the parachute pack still attached to their back – and free-fall to safety. Two lieutenant colonels did this on missions in Vietnam when SAMs exploded and brought down the B-52s they were riding in as Deputy Airborne Commander).

A relatively short flight in a B-52 is fun but flying for ten-fourteen hours, barely changing seats and without a conventional toilet plus only a small bunk bed at the rear of the flight deck (and unable to turn over) must be excruciating! I

Stealth

can only compare conditions to flying long haul, say London-San Francisco, wearing an oxygen mask, bone dome/visor, gloves, boots and flight suit and with a forty-pound parachute pack strapped to your back! Having said all of this, given a choice I would still board a B-52 any day of the week to fly Trans-Atlantic or even to Australia and back!

I have even been arrested for my art! Let me explain. It was on a cruise ship in the Mediterranean. Actually it was aboard the US Navy carrier *John F Kennedy*. One of the aft deck's four arrester-wires brought our C-2 Greyhound approaching at 200 mph, to a heart-stopping halt in two seconds. Moments before we had a few stomach-turning turns as the C-2 passed the carrier at 250 ft, banked sharply to port in a full battle break and sidled in for a pulsating, exciting few seconds into the landing pattern. Closer, closer, then thump! Many would like the photo opportunities a carrier embark offers but might not like the arrested landing. (In the C-2 passengers sit facing the rear. There are only two small portholes and you can't really see the deck so you can only 'anticipate'). And in 24-hrs time you will be facing backwards again while shooting off the bow cat from 0 to 150 mph in two seconds! Greaaaatttt! Who wants to arrive and depart by chopper when you can go by COD (Carrier Onboard Delivery)?! I knew what Jeremy Clarkson was in for when he was catapulted off the *Eisenhower* some years' later. The famous 'motor mouth' actually dried up for a few seconds! Mind you I find Jeremy very entertaining and he's certainly got guts. Outside loop in a spinning, spiralling Hunter! No thanks!

On my catapult launch two journo's almost bottled it. I think they only got back aboard the C-2 because it was the only way off the ship and back to Blighty. The older of the two (who had ducked out on a chopper flight from the carrier earlier) was shaking so much that he could not do up his straps. He claimed this was because he was wearing the wrong glasses and could not see properly! But there are no stewardesses on military aircraft to smooth and soothe your flight.

Major David L. Leedom (left) *and 1st Lieutenant Jesse A. Hildebrand at the controls of B-52H Cherokee Strip, Call Sign Scalp 95, of the 93rd Bomb Squadron, 917th Wing, Air Force Reserve Command.*

If you do not strap in properly (and cross your arms in front and sit in the foetal position) when the catapult fires the C-2 off the bow of the carrier the negative-G will shoot you out of your seat like a cannon shell. You will hit the seat in front of you, smash your jaw and break all your teeth. At least that is what we were told and that someone had suffered this fate the previous week. It concentrates the mind wonderfully.

I am frequently asked how do I get the chance to fly in such beautiful aircraft and get the opportunities to photograph the Lancaster, B-17s, Spitfires, et al. there are two answers – a long one and a short one. Most enquirers settle for the short answer, which is, 'I asked'. You have to know when and how to ask mind.

Another oft asked question is what techniques do you use and what are the secrets? Techniques? Well, you cannot beat experience so if in doubt, ask. That doyen of all aerial photographers, Charles E. Brown, is uncontactable so I decided, 'Ask Jeeves'. Dick Jeeves was a photographer on the *Eastern Daily Press* newspaper in Norwich. In the Sixties he flew in the right hand seat of an English Electric Lightning T5 and photographed another Lightning off his right wing without it being obscured by their wing. As a boy I always looked with a mixture of envy and admiration at this huge b/w masterpiece adorning the reception wall of the old newspaper offices in Redwell Street. How on earth did he do it I wondered? It would have to be virtually impossible to get a clear shot. Even if you remove all your straps (about ten of them) and twist your neck and body like a contortionist your camera lens would be up against the side of the cockpit canopy! Dick revealed that he took the photo simply by putting his camera over his right shoulder and snapped it pointing aft! The end result was perfection! (I was even more impressed when Dick, an ex RAF National serviceman, told me that he had got a

Flying Tiger from Texas

14

second Lightning ride because he told his hosts at RAF Coltishall that he 'wanted a second trip, just to make sure'!

I copied Dick's technique to photograph an ex-RAF Jet Provost Mk3 from another JP (and also the *Snowbirds* not too dissimilar CL-114 Tutors). Sure enough in one or two out of the series of shots I took I managed to get the whole aircraft in view without getting our tip tanks in shot. Actually, wing tip tanks especially with the RAF roundel in the foreground, can enhance a good shot, and on a later flight I did just that. (I also repeated Dick's second trick and I got another ride in a bomber people would kill to get one ride in, let alone two. Photographers! Never satisfied!)

When photographing propeller-driven or rotary powered aircraft running up on the ground and in flight, keep in mind 'fuzzy' props by using a slow shutter speed. Slow shutter speeds go out the window if you are being thrown about or get lazy and rest the camera on the side of the cockpit, especially with the canopy open in flight. Then an image stabiliser lens or even a few sandbags will not keep the camera still. Slow shutter speeds using hand held cameras do work if you are on firm 'ground', as evidenced by those taken standing on the rear ramp of the C-130.

At least when you are photographing balloons you don't have to worry about fuzzy props. However, keep an eye out for lions! I had always wanted to photograph a balloon from another balloon, ideally in Kenya with the Masai Mara underneath. Early one crisp morning I tried an air-to-air in Flying Picture balloons over Kent but they plopped into the moat at Leeds Castle after launching, one or two became tree houses when their baskets got caught up in trees and the elements dispersed the rest. We ended up alone with nothing to shoot at except an early riser who stumbled out of bed in his pyjamas, pulled open the bedroom curtains and stared startled as we hurtled past his house and landed in a school playing field nearby. A similar scenario occurred later in the Masai Mara (no second balloon – not the bedroom) but at least there

Yellow and flame-red hot air balloon 5Y-CAT. At sea level these balloons are capable of lifting over two tons although in Africa they only carry a maximum of twelve passengers plus a pilot.

Back to the Bat Cave Robin!

was the opportunity at take-off time to shoot the balloon. Its burner beautifully lit the black early morning sky like a Chinese lantern. At first glance it's not a shot that would seem to tax a photographer over much. However, you have had to fly 6500 miles to Kenya to take it, it is 0530 am, you have been up since 0400 and for near neighbours you have lions, cheetahs, hyenas and other prowling predators!

Secrets? Really there aren't many. Without pilots to create the scene you would have nothing to compose. Preparation is vitally important and a face-to-face briefing essential. Always eat a proper meal and take plenty of liquid too before going aloft. I had a lunch of double burger, chips and two fizzy drinks before clambering that afternoon into the unpressurized Jet Provost to take shots of the loop at 10 000 ft. The meal worked for me but it might not for someone else — especially if they suffer from airsickness. A fellow photographer, knowing that I had done air-to-airs in JPs asked me for tips as he was doing jet-to-jet for the first time. In all seriousness he asked if 'fast film' might be a good idea! Trying to keep a straight face I said, 'No, you'll both be going the same speed and speed is relative — anyway, jet-to-jet is easier as you do not have to worry about fuzzy props! Getting serious I said, 'Beforehand: 1, make sure that you have a good meal and drink plenty of liquid and 2, forget about flying in the 'big' jet and photographing the 'little' jet — do it the other way round. It all went in one ear and out the other. He proceeded to 1. Eat nothing. 2. Drink nothing and 3. Do press-ups (apparently to strengthen his arm muscles to lift the camera. Lack of food and drink and the press-ups meant that his air-to-air ended abruptly with a grey-out!

If all else fails photographically then you can 'cheat'. Seriously though, while computer software allows you to achieve practically anything with any image, none of the air-to-airs in *Airs and Graces* is faked.

The one 'assist' I allow myself is a fish-eye lens. A conventional airborne shot straight into the sun can be hit or miss but using a fish-eye, especially through the canopy, enhances the image more often than not. It is an exceptionally fine lens for photographing aircraft in the formation. For the *Snowbirds* flight I was permitted only one camera in the cockpit (and I had to take the strap off because in the event of ejection a dangling camera around your neck can be dangerous) so I could really only use one lens. (Normally I would have carried another in a leg flight-suit pocket but the ejection seat was 'live' and the cockpit cramped). I chose the fish-eye — one of the best photographic decisions I have made. The fish-eye is ideal for that all-encompassing shot when aircraft are potentially out of reach to your side or behind you. (I was glad I had not stowed a second lens in my trouser leg. At the end of the sortie I had to reach down while still strapped in to re-insert the ejection seat safety pin near my ankle but in vain. Finally my pilot had to lean over and do the honours with difficulty).

A fish-eye also enables you to photograph the wings and engines of the Jumbo jet and the B-52 from the cockpit when even a wide angle will not. Then there is the egotistical photo of yourself in the aircraft using a fish eye, which gives the impression that someone 'outside' took it. When asked who did take it I usually say it was the late Kenneth Williams, a comedian who in a famous radio skit clings to the wing of a jet aircraft on take off, knocks on the cockpit and says 'hello' to the stunned pilot!

Finally, if you have faith in your camera ship and 'target' aircraft pilots and the weather is good and you have remembered to load the right film or switch on your digi then you should be OK. If you leave your camera at home or forget to load/arm it, well that's another story!

Dressed To Kill

This B-52H of the 2nd Bomb Wing is undergoing maintenance in one of the two special hangars at Barksdale AFB, which permit side-by-side maintenance of two B-52Hs simultaneously. The fish-eye lens gets the complete picture!

ONE – Chocks Away!

Spit-Fire!

Cyclone power

Going up in the world

Smoke On – Go!

Shades of Albert Ball – SE5A taking off from Old Warden

Opposite: *Veteran and Vintage*

Sun 'N Fun

22

America's finest

Texas Raiders Over Corning Elmira

Enter the Dragon Rapide

Herky Bird

West of Munich we followed Peiffer in the turn. Darren Maturi the C-130 pilot applied 20 degrees of bank. Jim Carezas, the Sat Comm operator, reported to Mark Naumann the navigator that a fighter has reported 'Triple A' in the area. Hurst was still a long way behind, although it did not look it on the SKE scope. Hurst radioed 'We are 103 miles behind and gaining. Might just catch up.'

'Coming up on Innsbruck,' said Naumann.

'Maturi banked away slightly to avoid turbulence. 'Full moon out there. Means we'll be visible over Bosnia.'

'Yeah, could do with some cloud.'

'On the interphone we heard a chilling reminder of the recent shooting down by F-16s of three Galeb jets. 'Unidentified aircraft land immediately or I will have to take action. You are in violation of UN Resolution 836.'

Nothing further was heard. The pilots showed no more concern in their voices than they did before. Mark Naumann cut in,

'Twenty minutes off our combat check list.'

The C-130 formation headed inexorably into Croatian and then Bosnian airspace. Somewhere F-16 escort fighters were patrolling, protecting their 'assets' as it is termed. Apart from us there was another, smaller 'package' of French and German Air Force Transalls heading for their drop zone at Tesanj.

We donned our flak vests and light-blue helmets and clamped our oxygen masks on. My BA-18 personnel parachute was on the top bunk in case I needed it in a hurry. Thumbs up to showed that we were breathing oxygen, then the Herc was de-pressurized, Navigation and cabin lights extinguished. Naumann called out the time to the IP (Initial Point). Higginbotham checked the fuel gauges above his head.

WHOOMPF!

Naumann asked, 'What was that?

He didn't wait for an answer. 'Did we take a hit? Did any pieces fly off?'

Fortunately, it was nothing more than an air pocket.

Night Drop to Bjelimici
Martin W. Bowman

Captain Darren Maturi (left), and Captain Mike Brignola.

Opposite: *Stearmans strutting their stuff*

'Out there on the sod field stood the objects of our attention: rows and rows of beautiful blue-and-yellow Stearman PT-17s. Others were in the air, or taxying back and forth. We weren't long in getting acquainted. After finding our living quarters and receiving our flying issue – helmet, goggles, two flying suits and a parachute – we were divided up into groups of five and assigned to our instructors. Mine was Mr. Anderson, an affable, low-key southerner who, so help me, started us off by saying 'Gentlemen, this is an airplane.' We spent the first day hearing him talk about the basics of flying all morning, and learning to crank PT-17s all afternoon. The base hosted two classes at once. We quickly learned the essentials of being underclassmen: we had to crank the upperclass's engines.

Actual cockpit training began on the second or third day. As was the practice then, the cadet rode in the rear cockpit. This wasn't really a bad deal in the Stearman. I think you actually had better visibility and reference points than you did in front. That first day, the instructor showed all five of us where everything was in the cockpit, and what to do about it all – including detailed instructions about cleaning it out if you got airsick. We were told how and when to bail out (and not to do it accidentally, as happened once when a hapless cadet forgot to fasten his seat belt and hit rough air).

Then each of us was given an orientation ride lasting half an hour or so, never stopping the engine. Mr. Anderson showed us such niceties as how to do 'S' turns while taxying, so you could see what lay ahead; how to use the wind tee in the middle of the field to figure out which way the traffic pattern went; and how to find the field again once you were off the ground. All this good information came to us by way of the Gosport tube, a one-way speaking tube from instructor to cadet. If the instructor really wanted to get your attention, he'd hold the 'speaker' funnel out in the slipstream. You would get the full impact of the 100-mph wind right in your ears, which was no fun at all. In the course of the flight, we were given a feel of the controls, and a rundown on the various reference points on the airplane: the nose, the 45 bracing wires just ahead of the cockpits, and so on.

During all this time there dangled over our heads the sword of Damocles. The threat of 'washout' was with us for the whole eight months of training, but never was its hot breath so agonizingly perceptible as in those few short hours leading up to SOLO! That is where the majority of cadets washed out, close to half of the total who entered primary training. You were expected to solo after somewhere between eight and twelve hours of dual instruction. If you failed there were few second chances.'

Cadet David H. Rust, who solo-ed
in the PT-17 on 26 April 1943

Vibrator

'We entrained for Basic, at Courtland AAF in Alabama, up near the Tennessee River dams. That gave us a handy navigation aid; you could hardly miss the reservoirs. We flew the Vultee B-13 and/or 15. Vultee favored 'V' names for its planes. These were officially called 'Valiants' but us cadets irreverently and universally nicknamed them 'Vibrators' – I was quite happy with the BTs. They looked more like WWII fighters than the biplane PTs. You had much better visibility from the cockpit, more power, more airframe speed, and an all-metal airplane. Moreover, we flew the BTs from the front cockpit, except when doing instrument training. That required a blind-flying hood, which was naturally mounted in the rear cockpit. The main differences in cockpit routines were managing the dual-pitch prop and the wing flaps.'

Cadet David H. Rust

30

Moth at Duxford

In the eye of the beholder

TWO – Song of the Merlin

Hurricane attack

Hurricane pair

Opposite: *BBMF in all their glory*

Spit and Hurri

'I'd never seen anything like it. They were in two groups, one of about 70 and the other about 40, like two swarms of bees. There was no time to wait and we took up position and delivered No 3 attacks in sections. As only three machines at a time, in formation, attacked a line of 20 bombers, I just couldn't see how their gunners could miss us. We executed our attack, however, and despite the fact that I thought it was me being hit all over the place, it was their machines, which started dropping out of the sky. In my excitement, during the next attack I only narrowly missed one of our own machines whilst doing a 'split arse' breakaway – there couldn't have been more than two feet between us! Eventually, spotting most of the enemy aircraft dropping down with only their undercarriages damaged, I chased a Heinkel and filled that poor devil with lead until first one, then the other engine stopped. I then enjoyed the sadistic satisfaction of watching the bomber crash into the sea. With the one I reckoned to have damaged during our first attack, these were my first bloods, and so I was naturally elated. The squadron suffered no losses, but claimed six He 111s and two Do 17s destroyed, five He 111s and one Do 17 probably destroyed, and four He 111s and one Do 17 damaged, although we now know that in fact, there were no Do 17s amongst the German formation.

Pilot Officer Harry Welford, 607 Squadron,
Thursday 15 August 1940

37

Desert scheme

Opposite: *Now that's what I call a wingman*

Griffon's Growl

Lib and Lanc

Tail-end Charlie

Close Escort

Cadillac of the sky

'Blue Peter' of the BBMF, flown by Squadron Leader Clive Rowley MBE

'Happiness is flying the Lancaster at 100 feet over a group of Bomber Command veterans with four Rolls Royce Merlins purring away.
    A privilege.'

Flying the Lancaster *by Flt Lt Andy Sell BBMF*

Shiney in the spit

'At approximately 1440 hrs AA fire was sighted to the south and at the same time a formation of about 30 Dornier 215s was seen. I climbed up astern of the enemy aircraft to engage the fighter escort which could be seen above the bombers at about 30 000 ft. Three Me 109s dived on our formation and I turned to starboard. A loose dogfight ensued with more 109s coming down. I could not get near to any enemy aircraft so I climbed up and engaged a formation of Me 110s without result. I then sighted ten Me 109s just above me and attacked one of them. I got on his tail and fired several bursts of about two seconds. The enemy aircraft was taking violent evasive action and made for cloud level. I managed to get in another burst of about five seconds before it flicked over inverted and entered cloud in a shallow dive, apparently out of control. I then flew south and attacked two further formations of about thirty Do 215s from astern and head on...'

Spitfire pilot Squadron Leader Brian Lane,
CO, 19 Squadron, Duxford,
15 September 1940

Sizzlin' Liz

Paul Day slots in

'When all four Merlin engines had started and were up to running temperature, the aircraft taxied out to the end of the runway on time. Our turn came, Mick turned onto the runway, a quick 'green' from the runway controller and we were off. After a smooth take-off we climbed over base until I instructed Mick to set course for the rendezvous point, Mablethorpe, on the Lincolnshire coast, so as to arrive at the correct time to set off on the main route. A great deal of emphasis was placed on timing, the aim being to keep all the bomber force concentrated in a small area to prevent German radar picking up stragglers and homing Luftwaffe night-fighters in on us. In addition the effect of several hundred bombers delivering their load in the space of only 10 minutes was reckoned to have a demoralizing effect on the recipients.'

Pilot Officer Richard Hubert 'Chad' Chadwick,
Lancaster navigator 460 RAAF Squadron

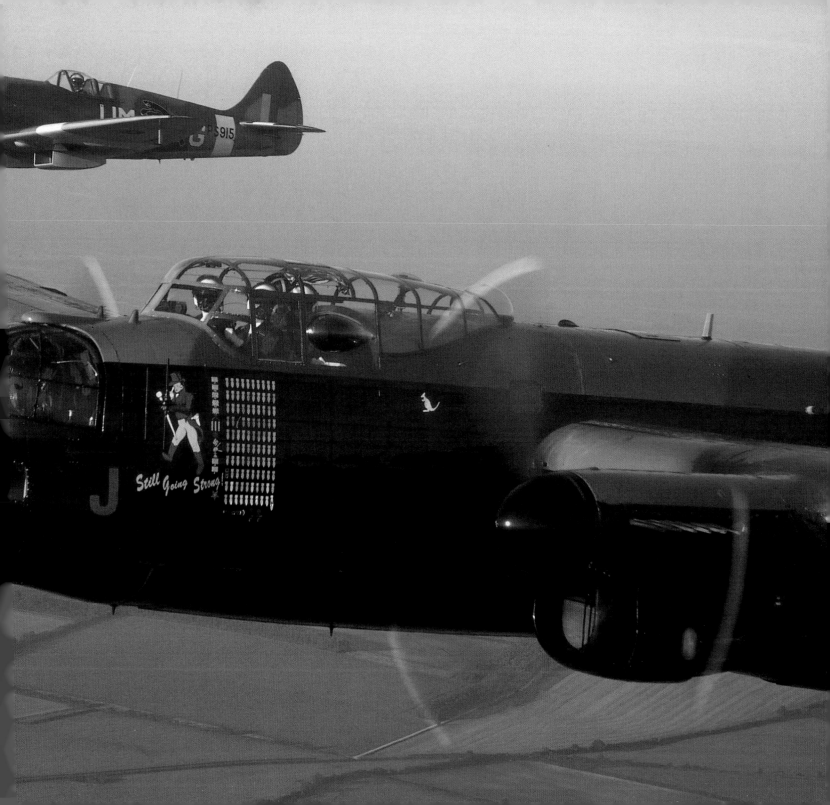

'Went to Essen last night. Briefing is always a pretty grim business when that target is announced. Price, W/Op, said, 'You faint and I'll carry you out.' We took a second pilot, a new boy on the squadron, to give him some experience. It was his first operational flight and he was still shaking after we landed. My boys are absolutely steady and normal under fire now, although we had never seen so many searchlights nor so great a barrage as over the Ruhr. It still represents to me a marvelously beautiful picture, especially on such a night with a few scattered clouds and the moon in its second quarter.

The sky was steel blue and everywhere below, there was the restless criss-cross pattern of long white beams, the bright pinpoints of the bursting heavy flak shells at our level, leaving big, dark smoke puffs that are often mistaken for balloons by the uninitiated observer, the long strings of red tracers from the light flak guns being hosed up like liquid corkscrews, the brilliant flares that hang interminably between heaven and earth and never seem to move, the photo flashes exploding near the ground with a piercing blue-white light, then the long strings of incendiaries being laid out in geometrical patterns among the buildings, and the great red mushroom explosions of the 4000-pounders. It is destruction on a colossal scale and terrifying in its concentration and intensity.'

Sergeant Robert S. Raymond, an American Lancaster pilot in 44 Squadron,
describing the raid on Essen, 13/14 January 1943.

Old Crow

'P-51Bs were much faster – you could dive out of a fight if you wanted to – they had great high- altitude performance, but we rarely went to altitude in China. On the minus side, their cockpits were cramped and hot (this was corrected in the D model). They only had four guns, laid at an angle in the thin wing. This frequently caused gun stoppages on one side if the guns were fired while pulling g's. We had only two bomb/tank racks on the '51, against three for the '40. And the '51 was much easier to shoot down because of all that plumbing near the tail.'

Major David H. Rust, 75th
'Flying Tiger Sharks' Squadron

'Streaming a white cloud of fuel, I feathered my prop and glided unmolested in the direction of the French coast, hoping that 1 might reach the water of the Channel and eventually be fished out by a German rescue aircraft. The sun shone brightly; the seconds seemed like hours. Around me, the bitter combats continued to rage. Damaged German bombers, British and German fighters fell away, smoking, burning, or breaking up. Parachutes opened or failed to open - it was a gruesome but also an exciting spectacle. I had never before been able to observe such an air battle. My glide took me ever nearer the ground; I would never be able to reach the water of the Channel. I glanced at my watch; it was about 1400. I was aware that this was the end of my fighting career and tears streamed down my face. I finally crashed my loyal Bf109 (into many pieces) near Rye, south of Folkestone and woke up later in the hospital, suffering from back and head injuries.

About a week later, I was taken by subway to the interrogation camp in London. The caption to a photograph an English photo-journalist took of me and my guards stated that I had quite a sense of humor for a German. I had cheerfully told the ticket taker that I did not need a ticket, as I had a season pass - a season that stretched into six year of imprisonment as a guest of the British King.'

Oberleutnant Jupp Buerschgens a ten-victory Experte of 7th Staffel,
JG26, shot down flying a Geschwader escort to the London area
in the Battle of Britain, September 1, 1940

Clear Prop

Black Six

THREE – Up, Up and Away

Bulldog Breed over Malta

Opposite: *Grosvenor House*

Two Stars

Lynx flight deck

Big Cats – Pumas on exercise

Hercules over the Severn Bridges

Chinook hovering in the Stamford Battle Area

Opposite: *Time to leave*

Yale streaming smoke

Spirit of Tipperary

The long shadows of autumn at Old Warden

Yellow and blue Yak 52

Skirting the Alps in a Swiss Ju 52

Flying pictures at Leeds Castle

Hi Dak

The eagle is airborne. As well as equipping RAF Fighter Command, Hurricanes were flown by three American Eagle squadrons.

FOUR – Flying to Glory

Icing on the cake

Tally Ho!

FIFI

Mary Alice

Lizzie

Flying Tiger

Two from Texas

D-Day stripes

Perfectly positioned props

The Road to Lincoln

FIFI over the Finger Lakes

Shades of Memphis Belle

Ace wingman

Diamond 'Lil'

Show Time

Indian Brave

Spit supreme

Reflected glory at Lakeland, Florida

Flying Tiger on finals

'We were told not to turn with Zeros, but I had the bit in my teeth this time, and I wasn't going to miss a chance. I split-essed with every-thing to the wall, and with every muscle rock-tight I was able to pull my pipper out ahead of the Jap. He was straight below me, a full 90° deflection shot, but I kept gaining on him in the turn. I knew I would not be able to lead him visually enough to hit him, because the long nose of my P-40 blocked my view. But I pulled straight through his flight path until he disappeared below my nose, then kept pulling until I thought I had enough lead. I started firing, for what seemed like minutes but was probably less than a second.

For one fleeting instant I thought I had overdone it and was about to ram him, but at that precise time, there he was! He wasn't fifty yards ahead of me, still at 90° to my line of flight, the red meatballs on his wings looking big as sunrise. He was still pulling streamers, and I could see the pilot's face turned up looking at me. I hit his prop wash like flying through a bomb blast, and only then heeded the voice of prudence and continued my dive. I looked back for him, but couldn't see him, so started a high-speed climb back toward the fight. I had better sense than to spend time and attention looking for my victim with Zeroes around, but the temptation was strong. I was positive that I had hit him, and longed to see a blazing wreck or a parachute.

'The Zero had clear advantages in ceiling and range but the P-40 had the edge in structural strength, diving speed, and firepower. I think the poor showing of P-40s versus Zeroes in the South Pacific was more a reflection of pilot skill than aircraft performance. The US sent green pilots against Japan's best. Certainly we more than held our own in China - not just the AVG, but their successors in US uniform.

The Shark had unboosted controls, meaning high stick pressures at high speed. But if you had the guts and the muscle, the P-40 would outmaneuver any of the other seven US fighters that flew combat in WW2: Most of us who flew P-40s under Chennault were staunch friends of the 'shark-faced tiger'

There were plenty, including myself, who loved the P-40.'

Major David H. Rust, 75th 'Flying Tiger Sharks' Squadron

Sentimental Journey and Texas Raiders over the Rio Grande

Blenheim tribute

Opposite: *No Guts No Glory*

'*My first meeting with the Thunder-jug was in late 1943 when I had trained with the 56th FG and joined the 355th FG at Steeple Morden. The Monster stood in all its glory, named Joker by its previous pilot, smelling of oil, gasoline, and in the cockpit, cigars. It basically overwhelmed me, the engine – an 18-cylinder brute – took up most of the frontal section and when started, vibrated the whole aircraft like it was going to destroy itself. After the engine reached operating levels it smoothed out a bit. To taxi this brute took an Act of Congress, 's'-ing was mandatory, but often one would almost leave the taxiway by turning for enough vision ahead. Taking off was a kick in the pants – brute energy in action. The giant engine roared into life as the throttle was advanced and it felt like an equally giant hand had grabbed me from the rear and thrust the ship forward. Overcoming torque was first line of defence against this monster having its own way. Tail up then lift off. A piece of cake flying this machine now it was in its best attitude – 'Airborne'. She handled very well, climbed like a homesick angel, but you had to watch out if you got her nose down. Then she would head for the deck like a rock, a heavy rock. It takes guts to dive several thousand feet and pull out. You think its curtains. No way can you get her level, but with trim helping, she does finally obey. If an enemy made the mistake of crossing one's path while firing the guns it was 'Goodbye enemy'. The deadly firepower was totally destructive.' While continually flying the Thunderbolt, it grew on you but I can't say that I ever felt completely at home in one. It was not all bad. I guess its meager range was really its only fault. I read somewhere that it was designed as defence not offence. That would make up for its poor points.'*

Pete Hardiman

Blenheim Comes Home to Watton

'It was not until we returned to our home base and we began discussing the day's events that I realized how scared I was. Then again so was everyone else and not embarrassed to say so. This was only our first mission of a scheduled 25 called a combat tour before we could even consider a return to the States. Each flight became more dangerous as the air war was stepped up. If a crew survived eight to ten missions at this time they were considered lucky. We were able to complete the twenty-five. I guess someone up there was looking out for the 'Worry Wart' crew. Perhaps our darkest day was 30 December 1943 because we lost a crew from our barracks. Men living together as closely as we did made us feel almost like family. To lose a friend and to actually see it happen was devastating to my crew and myself. Our morale was at its lowest point, especially when we returned to our barracks and saw their empty beds. We did not have time to mourn their loss because we were called out for another mission the very next day. It was about this time that I realized that this was a dangerous game I was a part of, was the glory of being a combat crewman worth it?'

T/Sgt Larry Goldstein,
B-17 radio operator, 1943

'As for the B-17, I am not ashamed to say that in 1944-45 I regarded her as a slow, flammable old lady who was really out of sorts among fast young friends, and-who became my potential enemy every time I flew a combat mission. Had it not been for the long-range escort fighter, the Luftwaffe would have driven us from the skies over Germany.'

Abe Dolim B-17 navigtaor

Above and opposite: *Radials*
Left: *Fuddy Duddy*

Cat on the prowl

Opposite: *Take Five*

Little Friend

'Compared to any fighter I had seen or flown, she was beautiful. I fell in love at first sight. Finally, I knew that North American Aviation had kept their word and given us the best fighter ever designed. The threat of liquid engine cooling vulnerability with the Merlin engines was only true if all coolant was lost immediately, some nursing was quite possible if the oil cooling remained intact, particularly in colder air. I personally nursed mine home from Frankfurt, Germany, with a coolant leak, about 600 miles. Going to Berlin and back in a P-51 was not the most comfortable way to spend one's day, but doing it in a P-51 overpowered the discomfort. The P-51D answered all of a fighter pilot's dreams, a wonderful flying machine, a view of the World around, a fantastic gun platform, and an airplane designed to combat all enemies, at any distance from base, and with a well trained pilot aboard a match for any and all comers. My only complaint was that we did not get P-51s a year sooner. Even Herman Goering knew he was licked when he saw B-17s escorted by P-51s over Berlin.'

Pete Hardiman

Mustangs over the Gulf of Mexico

BBMF Spitfires over the Wash

FIVE – Sea Legs

Opposite: *Lease-Lend. A Wildcat and P-47 Thunderbolt in close formation*

'The first early CAP was airborne at the time the Japanese were attacking Pearl Harbor, and exactly at the moment our Air Group was approaching for a landing at Ford Island. We didn't know it then, neither did the Japanese, but here was an American carrier only 150 miles from Pearl - fortunately, to the southwest -with its Air Group absent, except for a few VF-6 aircraft. Had they known this, certainly the 'Big E' would have been discovered and sunk. It was about this stage of our early morning operations that the Japanese attack on Pearl became known to us. Normal flight procedures called flight quarters about 30 minutes before launch. However, on this particular morning for VF-6's second flight, we got no warning, just 'Pilots, man your planes.'*

We had no time to really warm up our engines. As we taxied into position, one of the plane handlers held up a little blackboard. On it was written: "Japs attack Pearl Harbor. No shit."'

F4F Wildcat pilot, Ensign (later Captain)
James G. Daniels USN, 7 December 1941

Bearcat – scourge of the Kamikaze

Corsair and silver Spit

Corsair

'I was surprised and elated when my engine roared to life, at full power. Those 2000 horses made sweet music to my ears and the fight was on. The Zero-leader had now seen me and was manoeuvering directly toward me. We were coming at each other, almost head-on, at a terrific closing rate. I was ready for him. I placed my gunsight pipper just in front of him to allow for the proper lead and squeezed the trigger at about 500 yards. An instant later, his leading-edge machine guns spit flame as he exchanged lead with me. My tracers struck his airplane in the engine, and since every third bullet fired was a tracer, I knew he was getting hit thrice per tracer flash. My finger released the trigger as he flashed by, close under me. I never felt my Corsair being struck by his bullets and I had no time or cause to give the matter more thought. Before completing a hard left turn, I was in firing position to kill another Zero. I felt this was more important than trying to confirm the leader's destruction. It was almost a no-lead shot and my cone of fire blew him up with a two-second burst.'

23-year old Texan, Hunter J. Reinburg USMC Corsair pilot

Fat Cat Too

Navy Daze at Ellington Field

Its two PT6 turboprops humming, 'Spirit of Miami' waterskis past 'Song of America'

Amphibian comes ashore in Bermuda. Have a nice day.

'Coral Wings' - Lycoming turboprop powered
Grumman Super Widgeon at West Hope,
Great Barrier Reef

All the Aces. In the Mediterranean in October 1997 a VF-41 'Black Aces' pilot selects the full 20 900lb afterburning thrust that is available from the two P&W TF30s, and his F-14A Tomcat goes from zero to 150 knots in 2.2 seconds and hurtles off the bow of the USS John F. Kennedy *at mesmerizing speed.*

Tiger Tiger. F7F Grumman Tigercat on finals at Duxford

Alaskan Adventure – Beaver and Mars fire bomber at Sproat Lake

Bermuda Bound

Catalina making a splash at Fritton Lake

Tophatter turnaround aboard the Kennedy

Top Cat takes direction

SIX – Aces, Faces and Places

Spitfires on dawn patrol over Lincolnshire

Canadian Snowbird No.5, *flown by Major Tim Rawlings, one of nine pilots led by the team leader Major Bob Pashow.*

Vimy Ridge. 'God 'Elp All Of Us' passing the airship sheds at Cardington

'Baggers'

'1-2-3-Break!'

Opposite: *Fighters over Bomber County and Lincoln Cathedral*

'Mickey The Moocher'

Snowbirds *sun burst*

'We were allocated a permanent aircraft, QR-M, with the nose art of 'Mickey the Moocher', a real veteran, with 119 trips on the nose. {The nose had a Walt Disney cartoon of Mickey Mouse walking towards a sign-post upon which was written '3 Reich' and 'Berlin', pulling a bomb-trolley on which sat a bomb. Mickey The Moocher was a name derived from Cab Calloway's popular slow blues song, 'Minnie the Moocher'}. It was quite something to have our own plane, another milestone in our air force career. The ground crew was very proud of their plane and the number of trips completed. This showed good maintenance and a lot of luck. We hoped that the luck had not all been used up as it was usually considered that to survive a tour required about 70% luck and 30% skill. By this time Mickey was nearly worn out. The four engines were close to the hours for a complete change, the controls were sloppy, and she had dozens of patches on wings and fuselage. She took a lot of runway to get off the ground with a full load of fuel and bombs. We were the new crew given the oldest Lanc on the squadron but we were proud of her. I could sense through Mickey, the feelings of all the crews that had survived over 100 trips in this special aircraft, passing on their experience and good luck for a successful tour, a sort of feeling of comradeship and well-being which is hard to describe. Mickey was something to look up to, a guiding star. I get a similar feeling now, when, as a bush-walking guide, I lead a group of walkers through our magnificent Karri forests. We were allocated our new QR-M on 18 December. What a difference to fly. When doing our first air test with no bombs and limited fuel, I opened the throttle on take off and we were flung back in our seats. She behaved like a sports car.'

Flying Officer Frank Mouritz RAAF, pilot, Lancaster III
'Mickey The Moocher', 61 Squadron, 1944

Another day at the office

Super Connie

Air-to-Air? Helicopter heaven at Zhukowskij, captured courtesy of the 200ft high Myasishchev Bureau building

The Reds

Cool Cowling

My Mentor

Comrades in arms

Mentor in close

Get Carter

Chipmunk takes a bow at Shuttleworth

Thunderbirds Are Go!

Stearman Break!

Myasishchev VM-T ATLANT carrier aircraft at Zhukowskij (named after the founding father of Soviet aviation, and who also was an accomplished singer, and designer of the Moscow sewage system). The VM-T is a development of the Mya-4 Molot (Hammer) which made its first public appearance, over Moscow, in May 1954.

SEVEN – Jet Generation

Harriers at Old Warden on a summer's afternoon

JPs x three

Poles apart. Sukhoi Su-22M4s of the Polish Air Force at RAF Coltishall, Norfolk

No Step

Svasti Tovarich and das vedanya

Welcome to Mockba

Opposite: *Su-27PU Flanker at Farnborough Finale.*

Departing in Style

There will never be another

KLM Jumbo

Schipol Turnaround

Dambuster Tornado

Victor Vanquished

Aircraft Armed!

EIGHT – Finals

Finals

Stearmans in the snow

Gallic gall – the Flying Flea

Grief

'The Ryan PT-22 was of all metal, monocoque construction with open tandem cockpits. The wings and tail assembly were fabric covered and it sat on fixed gear with very rugged struts. There were wire braces from upper wing to fuselage and lower wing to wheel struts that vibrated and sang as you flew. You could estimate airspeed by their hum. We learned that those below the wing were 'flying wires'. They kept the wing from coming up in flight and those above were 'landing wires' to keep the wing from drooping down while on the ground. The engine was a 160 hp Kinner R-540-1, five radial air-cooled cylinders, one directly in the centre of the line of vision with open push-rods that let lubricating oil escape into the slip stream and onto us, causing dirty wind screens, goggles, helmets and clothing, it had a fixed pitch wooden propeller and would cruise at about 105 mph, was red-lined (do not exceed) at 180 mph and supposedly had a range of 250 miles or about two-and-a-half hours flying time I flew it on occasion to as high as 12 000 ft. Empty, it weighed only 1000 lb, with fuel and two pilots, 1600 lb. The wing span was just over 30 ft and from prop spinner to rudder, 21 ft. Students flew from the rear cockpit whether solo or dual, the instructor in the front cockpit. The fuselage was natural metal finish with a large black ship number on each side. The wings and tail section were painted yellow. Some had 13 alternating red and white stripes on the rudder, it was not hard to fly, in fact was a lot of fun, a 'forgiving' airplane of our mistakes, bad landings and such.'

Cadet pilot Philip G. Day
who solo-ed in the Ryan PT-22
and later piloted B-24 Liberators

Gleaming Dugan

Herc

Jungmann

Stars and Stripes - Ryan Monoplane

137

Stearman Sunset

Spam Can

Spitfire at six o'clock

Jungmann and Argus aloft

Check ride in a Yak 50

Silver gleam machine – Argus at rest

Moth to the flame

Go tell it to the Marines!

143

BIBLIOGRAPHY

A Yank In Bomber Command, Robert S. Raymond, Pacifica Press, California, 1998

Boeing 747, Crowood Classic Aviation Series, Martin W. Bowman, 2000

Castles In The Air, Martin W. Bowman, PSL 1984, Red Kite, 2001

Lockheed C-130 Hercules, Crowood Classic Aviation Series, Martin W. Bowman, 1999

Shades Of Blue, Martin W. Bowman, Airlife, 1999

Remembering D-Day; Personal Histories of Everyday Heroes, Martin W. Bowman, Harper Collins, 2004

Flying To Glory, Martin W. Bowman, PSL, 1992

The Battle of Britain Memorial Flight, Martin W. Bowman, Airlife, 2000